IN BAD FAITH

IN BAD FAITH

The Republican Plan to Destroy Social Security

JOSEPH NEWCOME

CPS Press LLC

Cover design by Joseph Newcome

First Printing, 2024

For information, address CPS Press LLC, 815 Pittsburgh Street, Springdale,
PA 15144

CONTENTS

| 1 |

INTRODUCTION

In the 2022 Midterm elections the Republican Party regained control of the US House of Representatives by a narrow margin. Republicans announced that one of their top priorities would be to reduce government spending. They blamed the spending on the Democrats and revealed that the targets for spending cuts were programs like Medicare and Social Security. Early in 2023 Republicans threatened to use the debt ceiling negotiations as a way to force cuts to Social Security. A few months later, prior to a meeting with President Biden, House Speaker Kevin McCarthy (R - CA) said that cuts to Social Security were no longer being pursued. Their demand was withdrawn, for the time being, and the debt ceiling was increased, but there was significant Republican opposition.

As a Social Security recipient, I oppose any cuts to benefits. I feel the same way about Medicare. And I'm sure all other recipients would agree with me on that point. Republicans threatening *my* Social Security benefits and *my* Medicare benefits got my attention. The position taken by Republicans to target Social Security and Medicare, and to try to include them in debt ceiling negotiations, was not smart politics. These are extremely popular programs. Republicans voted to increase the debt ceiling 3 times during the Trump Administration, so they can't say they are just opposed to raising the debt ceiling. So the question is:

Why threaten these extremely popular programs that benefit American citizens and voters?

Although I get Social Security benefits, I never knew much about the program itself. When I became aware of the threat to Social Security I started to do some research to determine why Republicans would target it for benefit cuts. What I found, and I think it's worth repeating, is that Social Security is an extremely efficient, and very popular, government program. Since the beginning, in 1935, Social Security has been a huge American success story. In 2022, 66 million American adults and children received Social Security benefits totaling $1.23 Trillion.

I also found that there is a current shortfall in the Social Security Trust Funds. If it is not corrected by Congress, Social Security will only be able to pay out 77% of promised benefits in 2034. The current situation was inevitable and is not Social Security's fault. It is a result of demographics, as you will see. There is time to fix the shortfall and there are many good ideas on how to do that. Social Security is currently paying out 100% of promised benefits. In my research on Social Security, mentioned above, I found no credible reason to target the program for benefit cuts. So, why then *is* Social Security being targeted? I discovered several outside forces directed against Social Security. They have been active for more than 40 years. Investigating those outside forces may provide the answer. I do that, in a chronological format, by following news reporting that documents Republican and conservative efforts to target, attack, and ultimately destroy Social Security.

| 2 |

A BRIEF HISTORY OF SOCIAL SECURITY

Before the 1930's there was little support for the elderly. Only veterans received pensions. But the widespread hardships experienced during the Great Depression generated support for a national old age insurance system.

On January 17, 1935, President Franklin D. Roosevelt sent a message to Congress requesting "social security" legislation. Within days Senator Robert Wagner (NY) and Representative David Lewis (MD) introduced bills to create Social Security. The Senate and House bills were opposed by those who considered it government overreach into the private sector, and by those who did not wish to see employers pay more taxes. A compromise was reached that passed both Houses of Congress and on August 14, 1935, President Roosevelt signed the Social Security Act into law.

The Act created an innovative American solution to the problem of old age pensions. Unlike other nations in Europe, US Social Security benefits were supported by payments into the system in the form of taxes on individual wages and employers, not directly from government funds.

The Social Security Act established a system of old age benefits for workers, benefits for victims of industrial accidents, and unemployment insurance. It provided aid for dependent mothers and children, persons who are blind, and persons with disabilities. It also provided funds for vocational training and family health programs. The Act generated complex administrative challenges: authorization of a Social Security Board to register retirees for benefits, oversee the payments received by the Federal government, and provide payments to beneficiaries.

The original Social Security Act only provided benefits for retired workers, at the age of 65. In 1939 Congress passed amendments that provided benefits to spouses and minor children. In 1954 benefits were added for disabled workers and they were later expanded to include their families. In 1972 Congress passed legislation for annual cost of living adjustments (COLA).

In 1975 the Social Security Trustees report calculated that the Old Age, Survivors, and Disability Insurance (OASDI) Trust Funds would have a shortfall by 1979. There are two Trust Funds: OASI, which is retirement and survivors' benefits; and DI, which is disability benefits. The Trust Funds need to be able to cover net outflows for 75 years to be solvent. In 1977 amendments were enacted by Congress that increased the payroll tax, the income amount eligible for the payroll tax, and slightly reduced benefits. But by the early 1980's there was an economic slowdown and the Trust Funds again faced short-term funding problems.

So, in 1983, the Greenspan Commission recommended changes such as a gradual increase in the retirement age from 65 to 67, increases in Social Security tax rates, and new taxes on the benefits of the wealthiest retirees. Congress passed these changes into law in 1983 and this law is still in place today. The current tax rate is 12.4% for OASDI, 6.2% for the employee and the same for the employer. The full retirement age is rising slowly to 67 for citizens born in 1960 or later.

The Social Security program is meant to be pay as you go. The current generation of workers pays for the benefits of the current retirees. But three key factors will make this task difficult. First, the baby boomer cohort is of unprecedented size; second, longer life spans mean longer retirements; and third, fertility rates are decreasing, which means fewer workers available to support more retirees. In 2000 there were 4 workers for every retiree, it was 3.5 by 2014, and the 2015 Trustees Report predicted 2.6 by 2030. As this continues the new contributions will be unable to deliver the promised benefits. The reserves in the OASI Trust Fund peaked in 2011 and have been in decline. The DI Trust Fund was expected to have a shortfall in 2016. Congress responded by passing the Bipartisan Budget Act (BBA) in 2015. The BBA reallocated portions of the payroll tax so more (0.285%) went to the DI Trust Fund instead of the OASI Trust Fund for three years (2016 - 18). The program then reverted back to the regular allocation percentages, which are 0.9% to DI and 5.3% to OASI.

The combined OASI and DI Trust Funds held reserves of $2.83 Trillion in 2022. But, as I mentioned in the last chapter, the 2023 Trustees Report showed that the OASI Trust Fund will have a shortfall in 2034, at which time only 77% of scheduled benefits will be able to be paid from continuing tax income. The report showed that the DI Trust Fund is forecast to have enough funds to make scheduled benefit payments for 75 years and therefore is fully funded.

There are many possible reforms that could be implemented to get the system solvent. One way would be to raise the cap on income that is exempt from Social Security taxes, which would bring in a lot more revenue. That amount, often called the taxable minimum, is currently set at $160,200 for 2023, and will be $168,600 for 2024.

So, how successful has Social Security been in living up to its purpose to replace wages due to retirement, disability or death? Social Security has been making benefit payments to retired and disabled Americans and their families for 88 years totaling $11 Trillion. Social Security makes an independent senior lifestyle possible. It is the foundation of the United States retirement system and provides millions of Americans peace of mind as they grow older. Social Security is also a very responsible program that anticipates liabilities, plans for the revenues, saves for the future, and has never missed a payment. Social Security's performance in carrying out its purpose can only be described as excellent.

| 3 |

PLANTING SOME NEW SEEDS

Republicans have never been fans of Social Security. When it comes to Social Security, history shows that the Republican Party has made repeated attempts to cut it, diminish it, privatize it, or all three. Republican opposition goes back to the earliest days. In the 1935 vote in Congress only 4% of Democrats voted against the bill, while 16% of Republicans opposed it.

The contemporary privatizing movement began with the Cato Institute in the 1980's. Inspired by the Cato Institute, Republican Presidents have attempted several times to cut or privatize Social Security. Ronald Reagan's efforts failed because of public opinion. George W. Bush's Second Term Initiative, aiming to cut benefits by partially privatizing Social Security, also failed in 2005.

The latest version of Republican efforts to cut Social Security began in 2014 with a statement by the 'Republican Views'. They declared their support for privatization and for benefit cuts to reduce government spending. Then, in 2015, House Republicans made a rule change that could have affected the benefits of more than 11 million Americans. There was no vote or debate, just a provision added, that would trigger a 20% benefit cut for disabled Americans unless there were Social Security benefit cuts or tax increases. Republicans said that the pending insolvency of the Trust Funds justified their rule change. The Alliance for Retired Americans called the action an attack on Seniors, disabled Americans, and the Social Security Trust Funds.

In 2016 the Republican Party Platform on Social Security sets a goal of getting Social Security spending under control. It talks about "creating wealth", code for privatization; opposing tax increases, such as raising the cap on the Social Security taxable minimum; and says current retirees are safe, which doesn't sound safe for current workers and is intentionally vague. And that is by design because benefit cuts are deeply unpopular with the American people. But we know where they stand because in 2016, as the party's nominee, Donald Trump said the quiet part out loud when he said: "I'm not going to cut Social Security like *every other Republican*".

Are these statements from Republicans about Social Security true?

Will Social Security benefit cuts reduce government spending?
Is the solvency status critical, requiring benefit cuts or new taxes?
Is Social Security spending out of control?

I will investigate.

| 4 |

THE TAX CUTS AND JOBS ACT

As I have said, Social Security is a very popular program, and it provides benefits to millions of Americans every month, many of them Republicans. So, at first look, it is surprising that Republicans do not support such a popular program. They are politicians, aren't they? Well, yes, but their reasoning is bound by ideology. So, instead of supporting Social Security for all the good it does, Republicans endorse privatization, benefit cuts, and reducing spending. The emphasis is clearly on spending. Social Security is spending too much or spending more than it should be.

Beginning in 2017 the Republicans controlled the Presidency and both Houses of Congress. Early in 2017 President Trump announced that tax reform was at the top of the list of the administration's priorities. On December 22, 2017, President Trump signed the Tax Cuts and Jobs Act (TCJA) into law. The law was the largest overhaul of the tax code in 30 years, created a 21% corporate tax rate, and cut taxes an average of $1,200 for taxpayers in 2018. However, the tax cuts for individuals and families will expire in 2025.

The TCJA was a big win for wealthy individuals and corporations since the tax cuts for them were permanent. Taxes were cut on corporate profits, investment income, estate taxes, and more. No Democrat voted for the bill and 12 House Republicans voted against it. The

Congressional Budget Office (CBO) forecast was that the TCJA would raise the Federal deficit by $1.9 Trillion over 10 years.

The Treasury Secretary claimed the law would spur sufficient economic growth to pay for itself. The Treasury Department released a report that projected increased revenues of $1.8 Trillion over 10 years. But the analysis was based on higher growth projections than the Federal Reserve had predicted. Many economists questioned the accuracy of the report, stating that it was more like a "thought experiment" than an actual projection of economic effects. The Committee for a Responsible Federal Budget (CRFB) argued that the Treasury Department was using "fantastical assumptions" to reach its conclusions. The CRFB also reported there was not one independent economist who agreed the TCJA would pay for itself.

In contrast to the wealthy and corporations, households earning $20-30,000 will be paying 27% more in 2027 than they would on the old tax code. Those making over $1 Million will pay 1% less. Promises by Republicans that low- and middle-class Americans would not get a tax increase came with an expiration date. The TCJA did not simplify the tax code or deal with the issues that concern taxpayers the most: taxes that are too low on corporations and the wealthy.

The tax cuts in the TCJA are called supply side tax cuts. Republicans have claimed for decades that these tax cuts increase growth and revenue. The theory predicts tax cuts to the wealthy and corporations will lead them to invest their increased profits. But this theory has been proven to be false. Evidence suggests these tax cuts have a very small, if any, positive effect on long term growth. What they actually do is create larger deficits and more income inequality. Supply side tax cuts are a risky economic policy, and place a burden on growth, as opposed to promoting growth, because there is no offsetting revenue. A review of current data shows:

Supply side tax cuts do not improve economic outcomes. The economy performed equally as well after tax increases in 1993 and 2012 as it did after tax cuts in 1981 and 2001.

Supply side tax cuts reward those who have already had significant income gains.

The economy does not benefit from corporate tax cuts - the shareholders do.

Lower corporate tax rates do not increase investments in the US.

Preliminary reports on the economic effects of the TCJA showed minimal growth in 2018. That type of first year effect usually tends to rule out any strong growth. Despite significant amounts of dividends paid compared to previous years there was no similar increase in investments from abroad. And data shows that despite large corporate repurchases of shares, little was directed to paying workers.

Supply side tax cuts and privatization are key components of an economic theory and ideology known as neoliberalism. This is the ideology that binds the reasoning of Republicans. It started in the 1930's and basically argues that market forces should decide winners and losers and corporations should be mostly free from taxes and regulation. Neoliberalism is presented as a viable economic theory, but in reality, was created by the wealthy. They funded Think Tanks to promote the theory, and its policies, to Republicans. These policies started to catch on in the 1970's but they went full blown in 1980 with the election of Ronald Reagan.

When you take a closer look at this economic theory you can see that it is nothing more than a corporate wish list disguised as something legitimate. It is all about the freedom for corporations to operate without accountability, and to avoid paying taxes.

The economic results of this theory are:

Massive tax cuts for the wealthy and corporations, so they are free from being required to distribute their wealth and reduce poverty.

Crushing of trade unions, so they are free to pay low wages.

Deregulation, so they are free to pollute the environment, expose workers to unsafe conditions, charge abusive interest rates, and design risky financial products.

Economic growth slowed down in the 1980's, but not for the wealthy. Inequality, in the distribution of both income and wealth, rose rapidly in this era, after 60 years of decline. According to some very distinguished scholars, the economic result of neoliberalism has been the greatest transfer of wealth in history. It has been estimated that over this time $60 Trillion has been transferred from the American middle class to corporations and the wealthy.

| 5 |

STARVE THE BEAST

The supply side theory, that tax cuts promote growth and increase revenue, also claims that tax cuts reduce the size of government. The reasoning is that reduced government revenues will put pressure on policymakers to reduce spending. This theory is known as 'starve the beast', and for many years it has been very attractive to Republicans. It is not clear when this theory originated, but it is uniformly rejected by economists as being inconsistent with the facts. Critics claim it has diverted attention away from valid political reforms needed to limit government growth.

The relationship between tax cuts and spending reduction, in reality, does not conform to what the starve the beast theory predicts. In President Reagan's first term, tax cuts reduced revenue from 19% of GDP to 17%, but spending rose from 21.6% of GDP to 22.2%. President George W Bush's tax cuts decreased revenues from 20% of GDP to 17%, but spending rose from 17.6% of GDP to 20.2%, and blew up the deficit. In fact, if you look at 4 major tax cuts going back to President Truman there is no evidence to support the starve the beast theory. Every one of those episodes failed to produce a reduction in spending and actually showed an acceleration of spending. So exactly the opposite has been true: tax cuts have increased spending.

So far, the starve the beast theory has been wrong every time. But TCJA is the most recent tax cut, and it offers an opportunity to see how starve the beast performed. If the theory worked, cutting $1.9 Trillion from government revenues over 10 years should result in less spending as policymakers respond to less available revenue. But as of February 2018, it didn't look that way.

At that point Republican and Democratic leaders were considering increasing discretionary spending by around $300 Billion over 2 years. The nonpartisan Committee for a Responsible Federal Budget (CRFB) estimated the deficit would surpass $1 Trillion in 2019, during a healthy economy. Starve the beast consistently fails to be a valid economic theory.

So, supply side theory has proven to be an illusion. Tax cuts do not increase growth or revenue. They do not reduce the size of government. They *increase* spending and *add to the debt and deficit.* If Republicans cling to this fantasy they pose a real threat to fiscal stability and growth. The starve the beast perspective has led too many Republicans to be casual about the political discipline necessary to control federal spending. They are counting on tax cuts to solve the problem.

| 6 |

HYPOCRISY

Social Security and Medicare are often put together in reporting. This book is about Social Security. Medicare and Medicaid are health-care entitlements, and they are separate programs, and their finances and Trust Funds are different. I will provide a summary of these programs in a later chapter.

On December 6, 2017, an article in the Washington Post included a quote from Senator Marco Rubio (R-FL), he said: "the driver of our debt is the structure of Social Security and Medicare for future bene-ficiaries". When he was asked for clarification Senator Rubio said he did not want to cut benefits for current retirees.

In March of 2018 Republican leadership in the House of Represen-tatives announced a plan to hold a vote on a Balanced Budget Amend-ment (BBA). The consensus among economists is that a BBA would be harmful to the economy, to our government, and especially to Social Security. I will cover the BBA issue later in this book. The reporting noted it was difficult to take Republican's concerns for a balanced budget seriously after their passage of the budget busting TCJA. The report stopped short of using the word 'hypocritical' to describe their behavior.

In October of 2018 Senator Mitch McConnell (R-KY) blamed en-titlements for rising deficits. Later that same month he suggested cuts to Social Security and Medicare were needed to reduce the deficit, and claimed they are the real drivers of the debt. The report on McConnell's statements suggested that they gave away the Republican strategy: pass a deficit exploding tax cut and then argue the real problem is spending on Social Security and entitlements. They also stopped short of using the word 'hypocritical', but it was implied in both reports.

On October 30, 2018, White House Economic Adviser Larry Kudlow confirmed plans to push for more entitlement cuts in 2019. In a 1996 Wall Street Journal Op Ed (an opinion essay), Kudlow wrote: "Tax cuts impose a restraint on the size of government. Tax cuts will starve the beast... Specifically, tax cuts provide a policy incentive to search for market solutions to the problems of Social Security, healthcare, education, and the environment". Notice the reference to market solutions, tax cuts, starve the beast, and the neoliberalism agenda.

In August of 2019 Forbes reported on plans by Republican Senators to make big cuts to entitlements if Trump were to be re-elected. The Senators claimed the cuts were necessary to reduce the deficit. Senators Barrasso (WY), Thune (SD) and McConnell were named in the report. They indicated the chief target was Social Security.

The attacks on Social Security highlight cruel hypocrisy on the part of Republicans. Now they say they are worried about debt and deficits and want to cut desperately needed programs for millions of Americans. It confirms their strategy to reward the wealthy and then take it back from the middle class and the poor. It's all part of the plan to continue the greatest transfer of wealth in history.

This review of Republican behavior between December of 2017 and August of 2019 documents numerous attacks on Social Security: it is blamed for being a driver of the debt; it is conflated with entitlement spending by design, even though it is not an entitlement; and it is threatened by a possible BBA. Social Security is getting beat up by Republicans in these press reports. But there is one fact Republicans don't want you to know. And that is: Social Security does not, in any way, add to the debt or deficits. Social Security can only pay out what it takes in and not a penny more. That is why, when there is a shortfall,

Social Security cannot pay all promised benefits. Social Security cannot borrow money. To say that Social Security contributes to the debt is a lie - they made it up. It is not about debt. Republicans do not care about the debt. Republicans only complain about the debt when there is a Democratic President.

This chapter provides documentary proof of Republican hypocrisy. They claim to be serious about reducing the debt, but they pass the TCJA, that added to the debt. Then, after taking care of the wealthy and corporations, they attempt to cut programs that help the poor and middle class.

There is also documentary proof of Republican misinformation. They purposely conflate Social Security with Medicare and entitlements.

And we have documentary proof of Republican lies. Several Republican lawmakers are on the record claiming Social Security adds to the debt.

Since we are on the subject of Republican misbehavior it feels like a good time to go back to those Republican policy positions at the end of Chapter 3. Are the statements from the Republican Party about Social Security true?

1. Will Social Security benefit cuts reduce government spending?

No, because Social Security does not affect the budget. Any cuts from Social Security would remain in the Trust Funds. This would NOT reduce government spending and is another lie.

2. Is the Trust Fund's solvency status an emergency requiring immediate benefit cuts or new taxes?

No, not yet. Social Security is paying 100% of promised benefits now. The trouble is the looming shortfall in 2034, when it will only be able to pay 77% of promised benefits.

3. Is Social Security spending out of control?

No, because we have learned that by law Social Security can only pay out what it takes in and nothing more. Social Security's spending CANNOT get out of control because it was set up that way. This is another lie.

All these lies were made up by Republicans to justify attacking Social Security. This behavior exposes an extreme Republican Party hatred for Social Security, and an appalling indifference to the financial well-being of Social Security recipients.

| 7 |

THE FACTS - EXPOSING THE LIES

When I say Republicans have an extreme hatred for Social Security, am I going too far? Well, let's consider the facts. Social Security is a very popular and efficient program that helps millions of Americans to retire. Social Security does good things. The only problem Social Security has is the occasional shortfall that will need to be addressed by Congress. So, for being an excellent program, with a history of never missing a payment in 88 years, Republicans reward Social Security by endorsing privatization and benefit cuts. They have tried to denigrate and scapegoat the program for years by telling lies and spreading misinformation. I say that translates to an extreme hatred of Social Security.

When I say that Republicans are indifferent to the financial well-being of Social Security recipients, am I going too far? Republicans have refused to work with Democrats to restore solvency to the OASI Trust Fund. If nothing is done benefits will be cut by 23% in 2034. It appears that Republicans don't care. If they succeed with their plans for privatization and Wall Street tanks, do you think they care? I say no, they don't care. They don't care about us.

In a previous chapter Social Security was described as an innovative American solution to the problem of old age pensions. Other countries had tried similar old age pension programs, but they were always set up to be paid from the government's general funds. Social Security benefits are supported by payments into the program from payroll taxes on workers and employers, not from the government's general fund. The program is set up with a built-in discipline: *Social Security cannot spend more than it takes in.* That is the current law and can only be changed with a new law. Benefits cannot be raised without raising revenue. Also, by law, Social Security must invest surplus funds in US Treasury securities.

Social Security benefits cannot add to the debt, but the operations of the Social Security Administration are funded through the Federal budget. This is a tiny part of the budget. Many special interest groups receive more funding than Social Security. Administrative costs for Social Security for 2022 were $6.7 Billion, only 0.5% of total expenditures. That cost vs expense ratio is very efficient.

Congress controls the Federal budget and spending. A deficit occurs because of overspending or under taxing, or a combination of the two. Congress is responsible for debt and deficits, not Social Security. And yet Republicans continue to lie to the American people by claiming Social Security adds to the debt. The term "the driver of the debt" is quite popular. And the old reliable "Social Security's spending is out of control" is another one of their greatest hits.

We must assume Republicans know Social Security does not add to the debt. So, they are knowingly lying about the program. But, by lying in such a way, they expose their intentions. The first thing to know is that Social Security is a target for Republicans. I don't know why yet. But to make up lies about something to justify attacking it shows an intention to destroy or damage it. The intention existed before the lie. The lie serves the overall objective to denigrate and tarnish Social Security.

It is a coordinated effort on the part of Republicans. They have even developed stories to prove their claims that Social Security adds to the debt. Here is one of them:

It starts with the argument that if the government does not raise enough revenue to pay those who are redeeming Treasury bonds, there will be a deficit. That is correct. Then they say that since Social Security is one of the entities redeeming Treasury bonds that Social Security is adding to the deficit.

But to argue that Social Security, by redeeming its Treasury bonds, adds to the deficit is absurd. Social Security is no more a cause of the deficit than any other entity that holds Treasury bonds. The cause of the deficit is Congress and the President, who cut taxes too much in relation to spending. The Social Security Trust Funds are owed money by the government, they cannot be blamed for causing debt and deficits. The story starts out with a true statement and tries to establish credibility but with a bit of scrutiny it collapses. They made it up, so they have something to back up their lies. They just hope their audience is naive and won't ask questions.

| 8 |

WHAT IS THE PAYOFF?

So, at some point, Republicans decided to target Social Security. I don't know what their ultimate goal is yet. But they are deploying their strategy of telling lies and spreading misinformation to justify attacks on Social Security. The attacks come from multiple directions. Social Security is accused of adding to the debt, engaging in out-of-control spending, and being bankrupt. Social Security is purposely conflated with Medicare and Medicaid finances. There isn't anything negative to report on Social Security, so they made up lies to give them a reason to target it. Sometimes they say they are trying to help. They are not. These talking points have been made by so many different Republicans and conservatives for such a long time that it appears to be a sophisticated, coordinated long term effort from the Republican Party platform. Like Roe v Wade, they are on a mission. But to achieve what?

One possible answer for the ultimate goal could be privatization. Any changes they would make that led to privatization of Social Security would be immensely attractive to Wall Street and the Financial Sector. After all, $2.83 Trillion is a huge amount of money. Republicans could get significant campaign donations from these financial corporations, they could get contributions to their Political Action Committees, and maybe even a get a seat on a corporate board. Some members of Congress may already be getting donations from these financial corporations, priming them for a future vote. Privatization also fits into the neoliberal ideology. But many leading economists believe privatization would essentially destroy Social Security at worst and make it less efficient and less effective at best.

Republicans talk about cutting benefits, but they don't really benefit from that. Any resulting surplus would stay in the Trust Funds and would not lower the deficit. So, privatization is what I'm picking as their ultimate goal. But Social Security is very popular, and they will have to denigrate and tarnish it over and over and over again. They will yell and scream that the system needs changes and adjustments. They will wait patiently for the slightest crack to open up so they can get their hands on the Trust Funds. And, although the ultimate goal is important to discover, at the end of the day what matters most is that Republicans are committed to destroying Social Security. And they would if they could. As I said above, they are on a mission. No, it's more like a quest. Let's observe their behavior on their quest to target, attack, and ultimately destroy Social Security.

| 9 |

THE QUEST 2019-2020

In 2019 Representative John Larson (D - CT) introduced the Social Security 2100 Act. The bill had over 200 sponsors and received the support of 90% of Democrats and 0% of Republicans. Republicans provided no alternate proposal. There was a Republican plan introduced in 2016, but it was never acted on. I will compare that plan to the Larson plan at the end of this chapter. After receiving zero Republican support for the bill, Larson said: "…Republicans want to cut Social Security and doing nothing achieves their goal".

Also in 2019, Senator Mitt Romney (R - UT) introduced the Trust Act. The Trust Act would establish congressional committees with the specific goal of crafting legislative 'solutions' for the US Trust Fund programs. The Treasury Department would identify any 'endangered' Trust Funds. Congress would then establish 'rescue' committees for each Trust Fund to 'restore solvency and otherwise improve the program'. If a rescue committee proposes a bill, it would get immediate review in each chamber.

The reason I highlighted those 3 words and 1 phrase in the above paragraph is because they remind me of what David Stockman, President Reagan's Budget Director, said in the 1980's. Republicans have framed Social Security reform as an attempt to save the program from "disaster", hyperbole intended. Stockman said that such a strategy would "permit the politicians to make it look like they are doing something *for* the beneficiary population when they are really doing something *to* it, which they normally would not have the courage to undertake". Critics of the Trust Act characterized it as a plan to gut Social Security behind closed doors and a way to cut the program without leaving any "fingerprints". Social Security advocacy groups described the plan as a way to *rob* older Americans of their earned Social Security benefits.

In May of 2020 Republicans proposed a plan to pay for Covid 19 Stimulus Aid by forcing Americans to borrow from their future Social Security benefits. Conservatives from the American Enterprise Institute and the Hoover Institute at Stanford University proposed allowing workers to receive up to $10,000 immediately and paying the money back by deferring their Social Security benefits once they retire. This is similar to a plan pushed by Senator Rubio in 2018 to pay for Family Leave. That plan would have been funded by parents giving up some of their Social Security benefits and was also based on a proposal by the American Enterprise Institute. These proposals were never adopted because the lump sum payments would unduly hasten the depletion of the Trust Funds and are completely contrary to how Social Security works: current workers contributions pay current retirees benefits.

In August of 2020 President Trump signed an executive order slashing funding for Social Security by suspending the payroll tax through the end of the year. Trump also promised to abolish it if he were to be re-elected. Many saw this order as an election year bribe, paid for by Social Security recipients. Republicans were silent about the executive order, which was widely denounced as a direct assault on Social Security and the Trust Funds.

Let's get back to the Social Security 2100 Act, introduced in 2019, by Representative Larson and how it compares to a Republican plan, introduced in 2016, by Representative Sam Johnson (R - TX). An analysis by the Urban Institute in December of 2020 summarized each program and the projected effects.

The Larson plan would:

Substantially expand Social Security
Raising the payroll tax and the tax cap (to over $400,000).
Increase annual revenue by 37% in 2065.
Increase minimum benefits to 125% of the Federal Poverty Level
Boost COLA's
Reduce the share of retirees who pay taxes on benefits.
Increase median annual benefits by 35% in 2065.
Increase benefits for all major demographic and economic groups.
Reduce the poverty rate for adult beneficiaries by about 50%.
Lift approximately 2.6 million adults out of poverty

The Johnson plan would:

Shrink spending and increase payments to low-income earners.
Change the formula, move payments from high to low earners.
Reduce COLA's
Increase the retirement age.
Cap spouse and child benefits.
Eliminate income tax on benefits.
Reduce annual benefits by 1% in 2065.
Lift approximately 800,000 adult beneficiaries out of poverty
Increase annual benefits 13% for the bottom fifth in earnings.
Increase annual benefits 16% for the next lowest fifth in earnings.
Reduce annual benefits 28% for the top fifth in earnings.

The authors of this report note that such a large reduction for beneficiaries with significant lifetime earnings could erode political support for Social Security.

This review of Republican behavior during this 2-year period reveals:

No Republican support for legislation to correct the shortfall. Republicans appear to have a strategy of doing nothing as a way to cut benefits in 2034. Republicans do not want to help Democrats fix Social Security.

Republicans introduced the Trust Act, which would have established congressional committees to find 'solutions' for the Trust Fund programs. Social Security advocacy groups called the Trust Act a plan to gut Social Security behind closed doors, and a way for Republicans to *rob* older Americans of their earned Social Security benefits.

Republicans proposed a plan to force Americans to borrow from their future Social Security benefits to pay for Covid 19 Stimulus Aid. They proposed something similar in 2018 to pay for Family Leave. These proposals were from conservative Think Tanks. This proves that Republicans and conservatives are obsessed with attacking Social Security to the point where they attempt to include it in budgetary issues for no reason. What does Social Security have to do with Covid 19 Stimulus Aid? What does it have to do with Family Leave? Nothing, but they just cannot leave it alone.

Republicans were silent in 2020 when President Trump suspended the payroll tax. This was a direct attack on funding for Social Security. They didn't even stand up for their own constituents. They don't care.

The Johnson plan, detailed above, would reduce median annual benefits by 28% for the top fifth in earnings in 2065. The report noted that such a large reduction in benefits for those with the highest earnings could erode political support for Social Security. That's the plan.

| 10 |

THE QUEST 2021-2022

In April of 2021 Senate Republicans introduced the Sustainable Budget Act (SBA). The SBA would establish, within the legislative branch, a new entity known as the National Commission on Fiscal Responsibility and Reform (NCFRR). The purpose of the commission would be to find policies to improve the fiscal situation of the Federal government. It mentions specifically the growth of entitlement spending and the gap between projected revenues and expenditures. The SBA would give the commission the power to hold hearings and get information from Federal Agencies.

It is notable that 4 of the 5 Republican Senators who sponsored the bill have signed on to the Tax Pledge, to never raise taxes, no matter what. So, it looks like they are planning cuts. These Senators opposed the American Rescue Plan (ARPA) that provided fiscal stimulus which experts predict will boost economic growth. They vote against policies that promote growth and they vote for policies that have historically been proven not to improve growth - tax cuts. Even worse, these policies increase spending. But they just can't let go of their ideology.

Republicans continue to target Social Security despite the fact that 85% of Americans aged 50 or over strongly oppose cuts to reduce the deficit. This finding is from an AARP survey in May of 2021. The AARP also came out against the Trust Act, discussed in the last chapter.

Urged on by the AARP, over 250,000 Americans have sent messages to their federal lawmakers demanding opposition to the Trust Act. The SBA is just a clone of the Trust Act. They both attempt to establish committees that give a handful of lawmakers the power to propose cuts behind closed doors, lacking transparency and accountability.

In July of 2021 Senator Lindsey Graham (R-SC) and fellow Republicans attempted to hold Social Security hostage by using it as leverage in debt ceiling negotiations. Graham wanted Democrats to agree to the SBA and the establishment of committees to look at Social Security in exchange for voting to raise the debt ceiling. This attempt to attack Social Security was rejected by Democrats and the plan failed.

In October of 2021 House Democrats reintroduced the Social Security 2100 Act: A Sacred Trust. The bill proposed extending solvency through 2038, four years, to give more time to come up with a long-term solution, and to expand and enhance Social Security benefits. The bill is very similar to the original 2100 Act except for a few key items. The payroll tax increase was eliminated and replaced with increased Social Security taxes on high wage earners. At the time it was unclear if there would be any Republican support for the bill. Social Security Advocacy groups uniformly praised the bill.

In December of 2021 the first hearing was held for the 2100 Act: A Sacred Trust. Republicans opposed the bill, saying it was too costly and only extends solvency until 2038. Republicans also said the language used to describe the Social Security shortfall overstates the severity of the problem. On the contrary, it is hard to overstate the severity of the problem. Of course, minimizing the shortfall situation fits quite well into the Republican 'do nothing' strategy. Republicans made no alternate proposal.

Also in December of 2021, Congress finally voted to increase the debt ceiling, postponing the next deadline to 2023, after the midterm elections. Any debt limit debates were pushed back until then, and yet some former Republican officials in the Trump Administration were already urging Republicans to use the 2023 debt ceiling deadline as leverage to force mechanisms to cut Social Security and entitlements.

In March of 2022 the National Republican Senate Committee (NRSC) unveiled its platform which proclaimed, among other things, that "all Americans should pay some income tax". This would be consistent with the Republican idea that non rich Americans are under taxed. In addition to the plan to tax Social Security benefits the plan proposes to give Congress the task to report on "when Social Security and Medicare go bankrupt". This is Republican propaganda and is used to degrade support for these programs. Another part of the platform pledged to cut IRS funding, and its workforce, by 50%.

By reviewing Republican behavior during this time period, we can assess their strategy and goals for Social Security:

It begins with their introduction of the SBA to target entitlement spending. Republicans usually speak of Social Security as being an entitlement, even though it is not. The SBA is just another Trust Act, with an attempt to form committees to cut Social Security.

Republicans clearly missed the 2021 AARP Survey that found 85% of Americans were opposed to Social Security benefit cuts to reduce the deficit. They attempted to force cuts to Social Security in exchange for raising the debt ceiling in July of 2021. That wasn't the first time Republicans tried to include Social Security in budgetary issues, even though Social Security has nothing to do with the budget. They tried to force Americans to borrow from their future Social Security benefits to pay for Covid 19 Stimulus Aid. They proposed a similar plan for Family Leave.

The hearing for the 2100 Act: A Sacred Trust, in December of 2021 confirmed that Republicans have no interest in fixing the shortfall. This time they said the severity of the problem was "overstated". Their plan is to do nothing, and cuts will come in 2034.

And in March of 2022 the National Republican Senate Committee (NRSC) proposed taxing Social Security benefits and cutting IRS funding and staff. So, they want lower- and middle-class citizens to pay more. But it's okay for their wealthy friends to continue cheating on their taxes and pay less.

| 11 |

MEDICARE AND MEDICAID

Medicare was created on July 30, 1965, when President Lyndon Johnson signed the Social Security Amendments of 1965 into law. The bill had a budget of $10 Billion. Medical coverage took effect in 1966. Americans 65 years of age or older were automatically enrolled in Part A (Hospitals), and 19 million people signed up for the optional Part B (Doctors) for $3 per month.

In August of 2021 there were 64 million Americans enrolled in Medicare. Medicare costs were $926 Billion in 2020, accounting for 14% of all government spending, and will be up to 18% by 2028. Premiums for Part B have grown over the years. The monthly cost is $165 for 2023 and will be $175 in 2024.

Medicare Part A is funded by a payroll tax of 2.9%, 1.45% from the employee, and 1.45% from the employer. These funds are deposited into the Hospital Insurance (HI) Trust Fund. Part B and Part D (Rx coverage) are financed by the Supplemental Medical Insurance (SMI) Trust Fund, with funds authorized by Congress. The SMI Trust Fund receives funds from the government's general revenues. The SMI Trust Fund drew 25% of its total from the general fund in 1970, 47% in 2020, and is expected to draw 50% by 2051. Part A is like Social Security in so far as the payroll tax collected goes into the HI Trust Fund. But Parts B and D receive funding through the SMI Trust Fund. So, Medicare does affect the debt.

Medicaid, healthcare funding for low-income families and individuals, is the largest source of Federal funding the states receive. Medicaid is counter cyclical; demand goes up when the economy slows down. Medicaid gets its funding from general revenues, authorized by Congress. So, Medicaid also contributes to the debt.

Republicans have a point when they speak about the need to lower costs on healthcare entitlements. But, after passing the TCJA, it is hypocritical for Republicans to target programs that help ordinary Americans. It was fortunate for current and future Medicare recipients that President Trump lost in the 2020 election. His budget for 2021 would have cut the program so deeply that critics said it would dismantle Medicare for future retirees. Congress should look for ways to cut costs that do not cut benefits. Negotiating drug prices, included in the Inflation Reduction Act of 2022, will be a good start toward cutting costs.

Medicare and Medicaid do not affect Social Security. But Republicans conflate Medicare and Medicaid spending with Social Security as another way to attack it.

| 12 |

THE BALANCED BUDGET
AMENDMENT

In March of 2018 reporting indicated that House Republicans were planning to schedule a vote on a Balanced Budget Amendment (BBA). This action was expected and is consistent with prior Republican tactics. After passing the TCJA, Republicans needed to make it look like they care about the deficit.

Most fiscal experts agree it is prudent to address the long term-debt. They also agree that a BBA would be unusual, and economically dangerous. Besides inflicting serious economic damage across the board, it would cause significant problems for the operation of Social Security and other important Federal programs.

Two BBAs were proposed in 2017. Both were proposed by Representative Bob Goldlatte (R-VA), chairman of the House Judiciary Committee. One of these proposals, HR Resolution 1, included constitutional spending limits and a constitutional ban on revenue increases. Some of the effects of a BBA would be:

No flexibility in fiscal policy to deal with a crisis.

Needed benefits would have to be cut in a weak economy.

Social Security could only pay benefits if there was a budget surplus.

FDIC could not react quickly on bank or pension fund failures.

Vital government programs would be hurt, Defense, Social Security

Fortunately, neither of these bills moved forward despite the fact that Republicans controlled the Presidency, the Senate and the House during the 2017 - 2018 Congress. They could have passed a BBA if they wanted to. And what that tells me again is: Republicans only complain about deficits when a Democrat is President. They just showcase these proposals as props.

There is another part to the BBA movement: an attempt to convene a Constitutional Convention to create a BBA in the Constitution. In December of 2021 it was reported that The American Legislative Exchange Council (ALEC) conference of state legislatures hopes to use Article V of the Constitution to call a Convention to propose new amendments, specifically a BBA and term limits for Congress.

But Article V also leaves much open to interpretation. Congress can set the rules but the last Convention, in 1787, disregarded them. It's not clear if the Convention would be limited to specific topics or issues, like a BBA and term limits. What is clear is that a BBA in the Constitution would be just as dangerous to Social Security as a law passed by Congress.

| 13 |

THE HEARING - PART ONE

On June 9, 2022, the Senate Budget Committee held a hearing with the title: Saving Social Security: Expanding Benefits and Demanding the Wealthy Pay Their Share or Cutting Benefits and Increasing Retirement Anxiety. In his opening remarks, the Chairman, Bernie Sanders (I - VT) said that the hearing was about the" future of Social Security".

Senator Sanders described Social Security as one of the most popular and successful programs in the history of the United States. For over 80 years, in good times and bad, Social Security has paid every benefit owed to every eligible American on time. And, since its inception in 1935 Social Security has never failed the American people. No recipient of Social Security has ever received a letter saying their benefits were delayed or cut. It has never happened. The Senator then promised that it never would happen as long as he has anything to say about it.

Senator Sanders provided the details of the current shortfall and then announced his introduction of legislation named the Social Security Expansion Act (SSEA). The SSEA, based on an analysis by the Social Security Administration, will fully fund Social Security for the next 75 years and expand benefits to Seniors and disabled Americans. How to accomplish this goal? It goes back to the title of the hearing which reads in part: "demanding the wealthy pay their share". The SSEA would apply the Social Security payroll tax on all income, including capital gains and dividends, for those who earn $250,000 per year or more. This would affect only 6.4% of Americans.

The Senator said the SSEA would increase Social Security benefits by $2,400 per year for both new and existing recipients. This increase will lift millions of Americans out of poverty. The SSEA would also increase the COLA by more accurately measuring adjustments by using the CPI Index for the Elderly.

Senator Sanders then documented some recent Republican actions and behavior relating to Social Security:

Earlier this year Senator Rick Scott (R - FL), Chairman of the Republican National Senate Committee (NRSC) released a plan that would sunset Social Security every 5 years, raise taxes on millions of Seniors, and jeopardize the guaranteed income of 65 million Americans who depend on Social Security.

A few months ago, the Republican Study Committee in the House of Representatives introduced a bill to raise the retirement age to 69 over 8 years and privatize Social Security by allowing employers to divert payroll deductions into less generous private retirement accounts.

Last year Senator Mitt Romney, who opposes raising taxes on the wealthy to strengthen Social Security, introduced legislation to form a committee to propose cuts to Social Security behind closed doors.

In 2020 Republican leader Mitch McConnell (R - KY) told a Bloomberg reporter that he hopes to work with the next Democratic President to trim Social Security, Medicare, and Medicaid.

In 2011 Senator Lindsey Graham introduced legislation to raise the retirement age to 70 by 2032 and index it to longevity.

In 2003 Senator Graham introduced a bill that would have cut Social Security benefits by 27% on current wage earners.

In 2015 Republican candidate Trump said: "Every Republican wants to do a big number on Social Security, they want to do it on Medicare, they want to do it on Medicaid". Senator Sanders said this was one of the few times he agreed with the former President, but he added: "we cannot allow that to happen".

SENATOR GRAHAM - OPENING REMARKS

Senator Graham acknowledged the importance of having this hearing, although he has a different view on how to save Social Security. He says his view is more realistic and Senator Sanders' view is a "fantasy" and accused Senator Sanders of trying to solve every problem by taxing the rich. He agrees more revenue is needed but does not say where it should come from.

Senator Graham proposes reforms similar to the Greenspan Commission, which increased taxes, and raised the retirement age from 65 to 67. But he avoided any talk about a tax increase by just saying that they added more revenue. He made several suggestions:

Wealthier people are going to have to take a little less to help save the system.

Younger people are living longer so he said they are probably going to have to increase the retirement age.

A third reference is made for more revenue, with no specifics. Then he mentions the benefit structure several times. It is not clear what that means.

Senator Graham used Four charts:

The first chart, Dire Fiscal Outlook, shows the US deficit in future projections. This chart attempts to conflate Social Security with the deficit. It is false and misleading.

The second chart, Rising Interest Rates Add to the Deficit, shows that the interest payment on the national debt is more when rates are higher. This makes sense but how is Social Security responsible for rising interest rates and how would any changes to Social Security impact interest rates? His chart makes no sense and is just an attempt to conflate Social Security with rising interest rates.

The third chart, Depleted by 2034, correctly shows that only 77% of promised benefits would be able to be paid in 2034 unless changes are made. But then it says: "the Social Security program will run a deficit of nearly $2.4 Trillion over the next decade". This statement is nonsense. Since Social Security can only pay out what it takes in, it cannot run a deficit. Senator Graham is calling a shortfall a deficit, that is a lie. But it is a way for him to then accuse Social Security of spending too much. This is another example of a lie made up for a reason to attack Social Security.

The second and third charts were uncovered only briefly and then quickly removed. Not much time was given to see the details. The only way I was able to read them completely was because I watched the video of the hearing and was able to stop the recording when needed. If you were in the room, you could make no sense of them.

The fourth chart, Inflation Rising, notes that the predicted inflation baked into the COLA projections was 3.8% and turned out to be higher, so COLA increases may be more than projected. This may be true but Social Security does not affect inflation and any changes to Social Security would not impact inflation. This is just an attempt to conflate Social Security with inflation.

These four charts are designed to conflate Social Security with the national debt, rising interest rates, deficit spending, and inflation. Apparently getting rid of Social Security would solve all these problems.

The truth is, Social Security has nothing to do with these things. And it causes one to question whether Senator Graham is really acting in good faith. If he were, would he display four charts that contain misrepresentations and outright lies? No wonder why he didn't leave them up long enough to be scrutinized.

At this point the Senator claimed to have the better plan to save Social Security, but he failed to provide any details about his plan. So, since he didn't provide any details, I am assuming he has no plan.

| 14 |

THE HEARING - PART TWO

STATEMENTS FROM THE PANELISTS

Nancy Altman   President of Social Security Works

Ms. Altman's statement key points:

Support for the SSEA as a solution for the shortfall.

The decision to expand or cut benefits is a matter of values, not affordability.

Social Security does not, and by law cannot, add to the deficit.

An overwhelming majority of Americans strongly oppose any and all cuts.

Americans want benefits expanded, and for the wealthy to pay their share.

Congress must address Social Security in the sunshine, through regular order, so the American people know where their elected representatives stand.

Robert Roach, Jr. President Alliance of Retired Americans

Mr. Roach's statement key points:

Many people on Social Security are struggling because the COLA has not kept up with inflation.

Some Seniors have to decide between food or medicine on a daily basis.

Many Seniors in financial difficulty are now depending on their children.

Strong support for the SSEA, because it will solve the Social Security shortfall and expand benefits.

Alex Lawson   Executive Director of Social Security Works

Mr. Lawson's statement key points:

He revealed that, since Social Security began, there has always been a greedy splinter group of people who actually hate Social Security. He characterized them as "Wall Street people". And even though this group is small, they never stop plotting, and today they have taken over the entire Republican party.

Social Security has nothing to do with the deficit or balancing the budget. Any surplus from cuts would remain in the Trust Funds and not go into the general fund to reduce the deficit.

After the 1983 reforms Republicans began waging a new type of war against Social Security. The main tactic has been lying in the face of the American people about what it is they are doing. So now you will never hear from Republicans that they want to destroy Social Security, you will never hear that they want to cut benefits, in fact they always start their attacks on Social Security with protestations of love such as: "I love Social Security, I'm just worried it won't be there for us in the future". The goal of all of this is to convince people that they are going to get nothing so they will accept less than what they are owed.

Republicans cloak their attacks under new monikers. They call it privatization, but it is just destruction, destroying Social Security. If President Bush had been successful in 2006 and turned over Social Security to Wall Street it would be gone. And it wasn't just Bush, all Republicans were complicit. As recently as 2015 Senator Ron Johnson (R - WI) said it was a shame that the Bush plan to destroy Social Security didn't succeed.

Senator Graham supported the privatization effort back in 2006. He has proposed a bill cutting Social Security benefits by 21% and raising the retirement age.

And Senator Graham's plan is not an outlier. The Republican party platform in 2016 stated: "as Republicans we oppose tax increases and believe in the power of markets to create wealth". This is coded language which translates to cutting benefits and handing Social Security over to Wall Street.

Senator Romney tried recently to get an up or down vote in the dead of night on the so-called Trust Act which would create an undemocratic, fast track, closed door process to cut Social Security. They know it is so toxic to talk about what they want to do that they tried to legally create a smoky back room where they can figure out the best way to rob people of their earned benefits.

Which brings us to the current Republican agenda as set out by Senator Rick Scott, the head of the NRSC. He wants to sunset Social Security in 5 years. Senator Scott hates Social Security and wants to eliminate it, but even he isn't brave enough to say that and calls it sun setting.

Maya MacGuineas   President
Committee for a Responsible Federal Budget

I began to doubt the credibility of this panelist immediately. She suggested changes to Social Security that "encourage economic growth whenever possible", the Republican code phrase for privatization.

She said twice that "there are tradeoffs between funding for Social Security versus other budgetary areas". Two of the previous panelists said Social Security has nothing to do with the budget. This is an attempt to conflate Social Security with the budget and is deliberately misleading.

She mentioned things like Means testing and Progressive price indexing. These are just fancy formulas that result in benefit cuts.

She claims the best proposal out there for Social Security is the Trust Act because "everything is on the table". That means she thinks Social Security cuts would be okay.

And her favorite proposal is the one opposed by 250,000 AARP members. She is clearly here as an advocate for the wealthy. She said: "You can only tax millionaires and billionaires so many times". I was not aware of that.

Shai Akabas   Director of Economic Policy
Bipartisan Policy Center

I also immediately questioned the credibility of this panelist. He used the Republican code phrase "for those who most rely on them". This is common language for those who want to cut Social Security by telling high earners they don't need it and transferring their benefits to low earners.

He was vague and talked about strengthening Social Security's finances (not sure what that means) and benefit restraints (that sounds like cuts). And he confirmed my interpretation of his code phrase above by framing reform as moving money from the top tiers to the lower tiers. So, his plan is to cut the benefits of the top tiers.

| 15 |

THE HEARING - PART THREE

STATEMENTS AND Q & A - REPUBLICAN SENATORS

SENATOR GRAHAM

Senator Graham began by endorsing the Trust Act and calling for a vote on it.

He also supported:

Raising the cap on the taxable minimum

Raising the retirement age

Adjusting the CPI

Reducing benefits for those who can afford to take less.

SENATOR ROMNEY

Senator Romney put up two charts. The first one shows the Trust Funds running out of money. The chart is displayed for 9 seconds. He then displays another chart which shows only a Washington Post headline, no article, and says: "The Medicare and Social Security Disaster that Washington is Doing Nothing to Fix". It says it was written by the Editorial Board, but there is no date on the headline.

Senator Romney directed several questions to Mr. Lawson.

Senator Romney: What solution do you have to actually solving Social Security on a bipartisan basis?

Mr. Lawson: We would ask millionaires and billionaires to pay the same rate as the rest of Americans and....

Senator Romney, (interrupting): I understand what your answer is, but what would you do to get bipartisanship, how are you going to get bipartisanship?

What this exchange reveals, is that when Mr. Lawson suggested the wealthy pay the same rate as other Americans (6.2% on all income), Senator Romney immediately rejected that. Republicans don't want millionaires and billionaires to pay the same rate as other Americans. It seems to be non-negotiable.

So, bipartisanship, according to Senator Romney, means Democrats cave on requiring the wealthy to pay their share. Then he takes it further and says if they don't cave, they are responsible for benefit cuts. This intractable position allows Republicans to do nothing and achieve their goal of cutting Social Security.

The quick dismissal of Mr. Lawson's suggestion is proof of Senator Romney's main concern: protecting the wealthy, such as himself. Because of his wealthy status, the Senator is less likely to be objective about possible solutions for the shortfall.

Senator Romney also gets in on the act of conflating Medicare with Social Security with his second chart.

SENATOR BRAUN

Senator Braun, in a hearing about Social Security, spent most of his time talking about something else. He conflated Social Security with entitlements once, the deficit twice, the budget three times, and Medicare twice. He called Senator Wyden by the name 'Wyman'. The only thing he said about Social Security was: "we need to keep at least what's there intact". His statement was vague, and it was hard to follow his speaking. It makes me wonder if he knows Social Security is a separate program.

SENATOR SCOTT

Senator Scott began by claiming he is against spending cuts. He accused President Biden of planning cuts to Social Security and Medicare, without providing any proof. Senator Scott conflated Social Security with Medicare three times, the budget four times, and inflation once. His comments were full of misleading statements and outright lies. He continually spoke about issues irrelevant to the hearing.

He admits to proposing that Congress regularly review these programs. Then he says: "as you know we don't even vote on Social Security and Medicare, which makes no sense". He wants Social Security to be part of the budgetary process so he can vote against it. Like Senator Braun, he doesn't seem to be aware that Social Security is a separate program.

Senator Scott's relationship to Medicare has a history that not everyone knows about. He is the former CEO of Columbia/HCA, once the nation's largest for-profit hospital network. That was before they got rid of Scott and settled the largest health care fraud case in history,

$1.7 Billion, and pleaded guilty to 14 felonies. He was forced to resign in 1997 but he arranged to make himself rich in the process.

John Schilling, a fellow Republican and former employee, helped to expose the fraud. He expressed concern that Scott "may have an agenda to change the Medicare program in a way that would enrich the hospital systems on behalf of the American taxpayer. I would also be concerned that his agenda could include eliminating or altering the Federal False Claims Act". That is the Federal law that protects whistle blowers like Schilling. So, given these concerns about his agenda for Medicare, Senator Scott should be kept far away from Social Security.

SUMMARY OF REPUBLICAN STATEMENTS AND Q & A

Reviewing the statements and questions from these 4 Republican Senators gives us an opportunity to assess their attitudes and plans for Social Security:

I learned that their perspective toward Social Security has not changed. They are still talking about cutting benefits and raising the retirement age. They are still conflating Social Security with the deficit, Medicare and Medicaid, and the budget. They are still resistant to re-quiring the wealthy to pay their share. One Senator accused President Biden of planning cuts to Social Security. He provided no proof to back up his claim.

Republicans are saying the same things they have been saying all along. They are still spreading misinformation and lies about Social Security. Don't expect it to stop.

| 16 |

THE HEARING - PART FOUR

STATEMENTS AND Q & A - DEMOCRATIC SENATORS

SENATOR SANDERS

Senator Sanders began by stressing the importance for wealthy Americans to pay their fair share. He offered the example of the Apple CEO, with 2022 earnings of $700 Million, who pays the same in Social Security taxes as someone who earns $147,000 (the taxable minimum in 2022). He described that situation as "absurd".

Senator Sanders asked Mr. Lawson a question:

Senator Sanders: Mr. Lawson, what impact would raising the retirement age to 70 years have on workers?

Mr. Lawson: Raising the retirement age is a benefit cut of 7% per year, so if it were to be raised to 70 that would result in a 21% benefit cut. That would hurt lower- and middle-income workers especially.

SENATOR WYDEN

Senator Wyden says there are two choices: cut benefits or save Social Security. He says Democrats want to save Social Security. They oppose benefit cuts or raising the retirement age, which especially hurts working people. He also mentioned:

The leading proposal from Republicans puts Social Security on the chopping block every few years.

Republicans have talked about privatizing Social Security for years. The American people have rejected these proposals. We need solutions the American people are for. He provided two proposals that have the approval of the American people:

A Billionaire tax with the revenue deposited into the Social Security Trust Funds would extend solvency until 2100.

The IRS has a tax gap of $1 Trillion because of funding cuts and fewer audits on wealthy individuals. Better funding for the IRS is needed to go after wealthy tax cheats.

He says these solutions ensure that we have some tax fairness and that we pay for what we want in a responsible way. He said he didn't come to this hearing just to say what he is against. (Like Republicans who have no proposal)

SENATOR VAN HOLLEN

Senator Van Hollen began by saying that he supports the SSEA and is a co-sponsor. He praised Social Security as an extremely important program that has helped millions of Americans. He calls the SSEA a good faith proposal, on the table, to actually do something right now. He criticized Republicans for calling for bipartisanship without putting forth a plan for Social Security. He believes that Social Security is not something to be discussed behind closed doors.

SENATOR PADILLA

Senator Padilla began by stating that Social Security has lifted more Americans out of poverty than any other program and is one of the most successful US government programs. But despite Social Security's success many seniors still struggle. He also made these comments:

Some Republicans have offered plans to cut Social Security, but he believes we can keep it solvent and expand benefits, and feels Congress has an obligation to do so.

He supports the SSEA, and believes Social Security benefits, which are earned benefits from years of work, must be protected, strengthened, and expanded.

Senator Padilla mentioned how efficient the SSA is, with administrative costs less than 1% of total payments. He spoke about recent cuts to the operations budget by 17%, and staffing cuts of 13%, and said he would like to see more funding for the SSA.

| 17 |

THE HEARING - PART FIVE

Stephen C. Goss, Chief Actuary, SSA

Mr. Goss is a member of the Society of Actuaries, the American Academy of Actuaries and the National Academy of Social Insurance. He joined the SSA in 1973 and became the Chief Actuary in 2001.

Mr. Goss presented the 2022 Annual Report of the Board of Trustees of the OASI and DI Trust Funds which was just released a week earlier. The report provides updated projections for the next 75 years. The SSA must report annually on Social Security operations over the past year and for the next five years, and to report on the actuarial status of the Trust Funds. This includes the ability to meet the cost of scheduled benefits with current revenue and reserves. If a shortfall is projected, the report provides guidance as to what changes should be made.

Mr. Goss said that this recent report extended solvency to 2035 (1 more year) and estimates that only 80% of scheduled benefits could be paid at that time. And even though inflation is higher than had been forecast, employment and wages have improved faster than expected, so they should cancel each other out. (The 2023 Report reduced solvency by a year, to 2034, when only 77% of scheduled benefits could be paid.)

Social Security cannot run out of money or go bankrupt, but reserves can become depleted and may not be able to pay 100% of scheduled benefits. Mr. Goss reported that the 75-year shortfall that currently exists equals about 1.2% of GDP, so it is not enormous, but is substantial, and needs to be addressed.

The Disability Insurance (DI) Trust Fund is in good shape because of less overall workers disability claims and is fully funded under current law for 75 years.

Mr. Goss gave two major factors that are driving the shortfall. First, an aging population and lower birth rates results in fewer workers; and second, an increase in wages above the OASDI taxable minimum. The share of workers with wages exceeding this amount remained stable at 6%. But the share of wages in excess of the taxable minimum rose significantly between 1983 and 2000, from 9% to 16%, and has remained at 14% to 16% since then. He says this puts a lot of pressure on the Trust Funds because those earnings are exempt from Social Security taxes.

The Trustees Report provided guidance to address the shortfall. The guidance recommends increasing revenue by 33%, or reducing benefits by 25%, or a combination of the two. Mr. Goss concluded his statement by commending Senator Sanders on the introduction of the SSEA.

Senator Sanders then asked Mr. Goss to share with the hearing his analysis of the SSEA, and whether it indicated the SSEA would correct the insolvency.

Senator Sanders: Mr. Goss, based on your analysis, would the SSEA expand Social Security benefits across the board in 2023?

Mr. Goss: Yes

Senator Sanders: Mr. Goss, would the SSEA make Social Security solvent for more than 75 years?

Mr. Goss: Yes

Senator Sanders: Mr. Goss, would the bottom 93% of American households not see any increase in their taxes?

Mr. Goss: Yes, our analysis showed it was probably closer to 94% would not see any tax increase.

Senator Sanders: Mr. Goss, so this could all be accomplished by wealthy Americans paying more in Social Security taxes?

Mr. Goss: Yes

Senator Sanders then thanked all participants and ended the hearing.

| 18 |

2023 AND BEYOND

The statement from Mr. Goss confirms that increasing the Social Security taxable minimum for wealthy individuals would accomplish two things:

Establish solvency for Social Security for 75 years.

Require all Americans to pay their fair share.

Senator Sanders understands this and the SSEA is an excellent proposal to solve the shortfall according to the guy who should know - Mr. Goss. The hearing previously described took place in June of 2022 and unfortunately Senator Sanders' bill, the SSEA, never made it to the floor of the Senate for a vote. And, since Republicans have the majority in the House of Representatives, it doesn't look like the SSEA will move forward until 2025.

On February 20, 2023, Keith Hall, the former Director of the Congressional Budget Office (CBO) appeared on C-SPAN's Washington Journal. He was the Director from 2015 to 2019. In reference to the Social Security Trust Funds and their effect on the national debt, he said: "so far the Trust Funds have not contributed to the debt, they are OK".

On March 31, 2023, the Social Security Trustees Report was released. As I mentioned several times earlier, the report stated that without action by Congress, in 2034 Social Security will only be able to pay out 77% of promised benefits from the OASI Trust Fund. The DI Trust Fund is projected to be solvent for 75 years.

In June of 2023 Congress reached a deal on the debt limit. It was suspended until 2025. It was no surprise that Republicans tried to include Social Security in the debt limit negotiations. But the Democrats and President Biden were able to protect it. This brings us back to where I started in the first paragraph of this book. After the deal was passed Speaker McCarthy made a statement that included:

A plan for a commission to address future cuts to Social Security
Referred to Social Security as being part of the budget.
Named Social Security as a driver of the debt.

He could not have been more predictable. Between 2014 and 2023 the news reporting referenced in this book documents:

The number of times Republicans conflated Social Security with:

Spending and the Budget: 12
Medicare and Medicaid: 8
The Debt and Deficit: 8
Entitlements: 6
Inflation: 2
Interest Rates: 1

The number of times Republicans attempted to include Social Security with:

Negotiations to increase the debt limit: 4
Covid-19 Stimulus Aid: 1
Family Leave: 1

The number of times Republicans have proposed Social Security:

Benefit cuts: 11
Retirement age increase: 4
Privatization: 4
Committees behind closed doors: 4
Funding cuts, Suspending Payroll Tax: 2
Sun Setting every few years: 1

This behavior makes it clear that Social Security recipients got lucky when Democrats defied the odds and performed well in the 2022 midterm elections. If the historical averages would have repeated Republicans would have begun attacks on Social Security. Democrats should expect those attacks if the Republicans have the majority because their objectives will not change going forward. They pledged to overturn Roe v. Wade and they did. Democrats need to understand they will attack, privatize, and otherwise dismantle Social Security if they get the chance. It is imperative that Social Security legislation is passed, to restore solvency, before Republicans have a majority in Congress.

Democrats need clarity when speaking about Social Security. They should be campaigning on Social Security. They need to be clear with voters that:

Social Security does not affect the debt or deficit,
Republicans are lying.

Social Security is separate from Medicare and Medicaid.

Doing nothing is a Republican plan for cuts in 2034.

The wealthy have an obligation to pay their fair share.

Democrats can be trusted to protect and expand Social

Security, Republicans cannot.

Democrats should go after Republican voters and
convince them they are voting against their own interests.

In addition to Democrats being responsible for protecting Social
Security from Republicans, the News Media also has a responsibility.
Republicans have opposed Social Security on ideological grounds for
years, but they disguise their efforts with phrases like "reform, save,
rescue" and so on, when in reality they want to destroy it. They have
a way of coming up with things that at first glance seem plausible but
have no basis in fact. They are just made up to prove one lie or another. They have been pretty successful in disguising their intentions.
It is difficult for the media to cover this complicated subject with
sound bites.

I told a made-up Republican story earlier in this book. The story
said if all Treasury bond holders were to redeem their Treasury bonds
at the same time there would be a deficit. And, since Social Security
was part of that group, Social Security would be adding to the deficit.
The story is false.

There has been another one circulating and it looks like the media
is dropping the ball again. This latest story has been put forward by
conservative Think Tanks that have a long track record of attacking
Social Security. The story is based on facts but then it diverges from
them. The facts are that the Social Security Trust Funds had a surplus
until 2010, and then began to decline. And, as we know, because of that
decline, there will be a projected shortfall in 2034.

So, Republicans have called the shortfall a deficit.

They say Social Security has been running deficits since 2010.

Then, they go back in time, to 2010. The story says that when Social
Security had a surplus that money was taken from the Trust Funds

and put into the General Fund and spent by the government. Social Security received Treasury bonds in return.

Then, finally, they say when Social Security redeems those Treasury bonds, the government has to borrow and that adds to the deficit.

It is a story made up to trick people into believing that Social Security adds to the deficit. It exists for no other purpose and contains not one fact. Everything in the story is a lie:

A shortfall is not a deficit.

Social Security cannot run a deficit.

No money was taken from the Trust Funds, Social Security cannot lend money.

Social Security is owed money and cannot be blamed for deficits.

In one week, I saw this story reported three times, either in online reporting, or on cable news. This is just more Republican propaganda. And, unfortunately, a few news outlets have put out the fabrications from these conservative operations, falling for their lies. Social Security is complicated, but it is not rocket science, news outlets need to up their game if more sophistication is required to report the truth. Republicans and conservatives are going to continue to lie about Social Security and those lies need to be exposed.

In August of 2023 there was reporting that 82% of voters oppose Social Security cuts for Americans under age 50. The poll also found 72% of voters were less likely to vote for a candidate who supports cutting future Social Security benefits. And 77% approve of tax hikes on the wealthy to solve the Social Security shortfall.

The report also mentioned that House Republicans were currently fighting for funding cuts to the SSA that would "devastate the agency's ability to serve the American public", according to one official from the American Federation of Government Employees.

What I learned by writing this book is that there is nothing wrong with Social Security. The current shortfall in the OASI Trust Fund is due to demographic changes resulting in fewer workers paying into the system. But it is also due to a tax structure that benefits the wealthy over ordinary citizens. They need to pay 6.2% like we do.

Earlier in this book I chose privatization as the primary Republican objective for Social Security. I was wrong. Privatization is on the table for sure, but the primary objective is simply to protect the wealthy from paying their fair share. Washington, D.C. is home to an entire industry of Think Tanks, funded by the wealthy, who hire lawyers and ex-government officials, so they appear to be legitimate. The strategy is to make a lot of noise and attack Social Security by spreading lies and misinformation. They hope that distracts people from looking at the real problem: the wealthy not paying their fair share.

The Title of this book is 'In Bad Faith'. Have I provided proof that Republicans are acting in bad faith regarding Social Security? I believe so, Republicans have:

No plan to address the shortfall.

Refused to negotiate on any proposals by Democrats.

Done nothing, likely a strategy for 2034.

Hypocritically blamed the deficit on Social Security,
after passing the TCJA.

Called for bipartisanship as long as the wealthy are off limits.

The subtitle is 'The Republican Plan to Destroy Social Security'. Have I provided proof of a Republican plan to destroy Social Security? Again, I believe I have. Republicans have:

Promoted privatization, experts call it destruction.

Spread lies about Social Security spending to make cuts.

Attempted to include Social Security in unrelated budgetary issues to force cuts.

Continued to call for committees behind closed doors to cut Social Security

Started a fight for funding cuts that a report said would "devastate" the SSA.

It is now late in 2023, and the calls for committees to look at Social Security just keep on coming. Of course, these committees will be made up of current members of Congress. These people are, by and large, very wealthy compared to the average American. What is the chance that they would decide to raise taxes on themselves in order to fix Social Security? I believe there is no chance they will do that. They would destroy Social Security in favor of the wealthy. This is one of the most obvious conflicts of interest anyone can think of. These committees must never happen.

As I am wrapping up this book, timed to coincide with the end of 2023, I have been given a holiday gift. Social Security's longtime nemesis, the American Enterprise Institute, published an Op Ed that also ran in the Wall Street Journal. One of the authors is Phil Gramm, a former Republican Senator from Texas. Gramm has been called an "outspoken champion of financial deregulation". That tells me all I need to know.

The essay starts with this statement: "Americans imagine that the Social Security benefits they are promised belong to them". With the use of the word "imagine", it is implied that they do not. He also makes the case that Social Security taxes should be treated like any other revenue and available for government spending, not reserved for retirees. But that is not the law that was passed. Social Security taxes *are* reserved for retirees. So, he doesn't agree with the law that was passed - who cares!

He claims, that by 1939, Social Security revenue was being spent on the New Deal social programs. I doubt that, since Social Security is a closed system. He provided no reference to prove his claim that I could see. He may have just made it up.

He also says that only a *hypothetical or imaginary* accounting of the Social Security surplus was recorded. I wonder if he's heard of the yearly Social Security Trustees Report and the requirement for Social Security to purchase US Treasury Securities with all surplus funds. I'll bet there is a record of that.

I stopped reading after three paragraphs because I did not want to subscribe to a publication that puts out this garbage and gobbledygook. I can tell where the authors are going, and it is a novel approach. It is a straight up, slap in the face statement to Social Security recipients: 'the Social Security benefits you have been promised don't belong to you, and we should just be able to spend that money'. Why would they say such a thing? Because the wealthy donors who fund their Think Tanks want them to try anything and everything that may help protect them from having to pay their fair share of 6.2%.

This opinion essay is not going to change anything about Social Security. The author will probably suggest some form of privatization. But it is more proof of how the American Enterprise Institute, and other conservative Think Tanks, keep coming up with pathetic and baseless attacks on Social Security at the direction of the wealthy.

The biggest problem for Social Security is Republicans. They are the ones standing in the way of making Social Security solvent. So, the best thing for Social Security would be for everyone to vote Democratic. Certainly, every Social Security recipient should vote Democratic, even if you are a Republican. If you read this book you need to get out and vote for Democrats in 2024, and in every election after that, to ensure the solvency of Social Security. Oh, and don't forget to tell your friends to do the same.

| 19 |

BIBLIOGRAPHY

CHAPTER ONE

Social Security Administration   Board of Trustees Report 2023 (3/31/2023)   Press Release

CHAPTER TWO

The Social Security Act of 1935   (February 2022)   National Archives

A Brief History of Social Security   (10/27/2015)   Wade Pfau   Forbes

CHAPTER THREE

Republican Views on Social Security   (5/7/2014) www.Republicanviews.org

First Target for House Republicans? Cutting Social Security (1/7/2015) AFL-CIO Mike Hall

Republican Party Platform on Social Security (2016) www.greemantoomey.com

Trump's Second Term Plan for Social Security (8/23/2019) Forbes Teresa Ghilarducci

CHAPTER FOUR

Treasury Department Assumes... (12/11/2017) Committee for a Responsible Federal Budget (CRFB)

CRFB Reaction to Senate Tax Bill (12/1/2017) CRFB

Explaining the Trump Tax Reform Plan (2/9/2022) Investopedia David Floyd

Starving the Beast? TCJA Seems to be Feeding It (2/6/2018) Tax Policy Center Howard Gleckman

Supply Side Follies (10/26/2017) Center for American Progress Christian Weller

Republican Senators Push Social Security & Medicare Cuts (4/16/2021) Forbes Christian Weller

Neoliberalism - The Ideology at the Root of ... (4/15/2016) The Guardian George Monbiot

C-SPAN *In Depth* (4/3/2022) Noam Chomsky

CHAPTER FIVE

Limiting Government: Failure of Starve the Beast (2006) Niskanen Center William A. Niskanen

Starving the Beast? (2/6/2018) Tax Policy Center H. Gleckman

Budget Deal Will Bring Back Trillion Dollar Deficits... (2/7/2018) CRFB

Starve the Beast Enables the Bankrupt in Chief (5/10/2017) Niskanen Center Will Wilkinson

CHAPTER SIX

Why So Many People (Mistakenly) Believe Social Security Adds to the Deficit (6/20/2019) Forbes Teresa Ghilarducci

SSA Board of Trustees Annual Report 2023 (3/31/2023) Press Release

CHAPTER SEVEN

Ryan Says Republicans to Target Welfare, Medicare, Medicaid Spending in 2018 (12/6/2017) Washington Post Jeff Stein

A Constitutional Balanced Budget Amendment Poses Serious Risks (3/16/2018) Center on Budget and Policy Priorities Richard Kogan

McConnell Blames Entitlements, Not GOP for Rising Deficits (10/16/2018) Bloomberg

The Deficit is Rising, So Republicans Want to Cut Social Security & Medicare (10/17/2018)   VOX   Dylan Scott

GOP Revives Medicare Scare Tactics As Election Nears (10/30/2018) NPR Julie Rovner

Cut Taxes, Starve the Beast (9/30/1996) The Wall Street Journal Lawrence Kudlow

Trump's Second Term Plan   (8/23/2019)   Forbes T. Ghilarducci

CHAPTER NINE

Republicans Pushing Myths About Social Security (8/26/2019) Forbes Nancy Altman

Trump Just Gave Away the Republican Game on Social Security & Medicare (1/23/2020) Washington Post Helaine Olen

GOP Plot to Gut Social Security Behind Closed Doors Gains Steam in Senate Covid 19 Talks   (5/22/2020)   Common Dreams   Jake Johnson

Republicans Seek to Exploit Covid 19 Crisis to Cut Social Security Benefits (5/11/2020) Los Angeles Times Michael Hiltzik

Trump Administration Seeks Permanent Cuts in Social Security Funding (8/21/2020) IBEW Media Center

Comparing Democrat & Republican Approaches to Fixing Social Security: An Analysis of the Larson and Johnson Bills   (12/2020) Urban Institute   Richard W. Johnson and Karen E. Smith

CHAPTER TEN

Senate Republicans Push for National Commission to Balance the Budget After Massive Covid Relief   (4/15/2021)   Washington Examiner   Nihal Krishan

Older Americans Oppose Social Security, Medicare Cuts to Fix Federal Debt   (5/26/2021)   AARP   Dena Bunis

GOP Plot to Gut Social Security   (5/22/2020)   Common Dreams   Jake Johnson

Democrats Urged to Reject Latest GOP Attempt to Hold Social Security Hostage   (7/21/2021)   Common Dreams   Jake Johnson

Congress Has a New Plan to Fix Social Security, How it Would Change Benefits   (10/26/2021)   CNBC   Lorie Konish

Social Security Reform Bill Runs Into GOP Opposition (12/7/2021)   Financial Planning   Tobias Salinger

Congress Votes to Raise the Debt Ceiling   (12/15/2021)   NPR   Kelsey Snell

Social Security Fixes Could Animate Post Mid Term Agenda (2/22/2022)   Roll Call   Peter Cohn

The Not so Secret Republican Plan to Raise Taxes   (3/2/2022) Frederick News Post   Matthew Yglesias

CHAPTER ELEVEN

A Brief History of Medicare in America   (2021)
MedicareResources.org

A Brief History of Medicare (1/21/2021) Insurance Neighbor

An Overview of Medicare (2/13/2019) Kaiser Family Foundation

President Trump's Budget Would Hurt People With Disabilities and Dismantle Medicare (2/13/2020) Center on Budget and Policy Priorities Kathleen Romig

CHAPTER TWELVE

Balanced Budget Amendment (2/16/2018) Center on Budget R. Kogan

Conservatives Prepare New Push for Constitutional Convention (12/8/2021) The Hill Reid Wilson

CHAPTER THIRTEEN

Saving Social Security: Expanding Benefits and Demanding the Wealthy Pay Their Share or Cutting Benefits and Increasing Retirement Anxiety (6/9/2022) U.S. Senate Budget Committee Hearing www.budget.senate.gov

CHAPTER FOURTEEN

Saving Social Security (6/9/2022) U.S. Senate Budget Committee
www.budget.senate.gov

Letter to Edgar Newton Eisenhower by President Dwight D. Eisenhower (11/8/1954) Teaching American History Ashbrook Center
at Ashland University

Means Testing Social Security: Breaking Faith With American
Workers (10/25/2022) National Committee to Preserve Social Security & Medicare (NCPSSM)

Progressive Price Indexing Would Significantly Cut Social Security
Benefits for Many Recipients (11/17/2010) Center on Budget Kathy
Ruffing and Paul N Van De Water

CHAPTER FIFTEEN

Saving Social Security (6/9/2022) U.S. Senate Budget Committee
www.budget.senate.gov

Democrats: Medicare Fraud is 'Fungus' Scott Will Never Get Rid
Of (8/30/2018) POLITICO Aleandra Glorioso and Marc Caputo

CHAPTER SIXTEEN

Saving Social Security (6/9/2022) U.S. Senate Budget Committee
www.budget.senate.gov

CHAPTER SEVENTEEN

Saving Social Security (6/9/2022) U.S. Senate Budget Committee www.budget.senate.gov

CHAPTER EIGHTEEN

McCarthy Says Biden Stopped Him From Cutting Social Security and Medicare (6/1/2023) Emily Singer TIA News

Fact Check: Social Security Does Contribute to the Federal Deficit and National Debt (2/8/2023) Sudiksha Kochi USA Today

82% of Voters Oppose GOP Push to Cut Social Security for Americans Under 50: Poll (8/2/2023) Jessica Corbett Common Dreams

Social Security Was Doomed From the Start (12/20/2023) Phil Gramm and Mike Solon American Enterprise Institute

AUTHOR BIOGRAPHY

Joseph Newcome

A change in political leadership led Joseph Newcome to a shocking revelation: Social Security is under attack. What he discovered resulted in the writing of his first book, titled: *In Bad Faith: The Republican Plan to Destroy Social Security.* To Joseph it's personal, he is a Social Security recipient and does not want to see benefit cuts for himself or others. The book is an attempt to expose Republican attacks on Social Security before it is too late (like Roe v Wade). Everyone who receives Social Security benefits now or who will in the future will benefit from the information in this book and hopefully it will motivate all citizens to vote to protect Social Security.